FRIGHTENING TOYS

Charles Simic was born in 1938 in Yugoslavia, and is now Professor of English at the University of New Hampshire. He has won many awards, including the MacArthur Foundation Fellowship and a Pulitzer Prize.

GW00566773

by the same author
(US publications)

HOTEL INSOMNIA
THE BOOK OF GODS AND DEVILS
THE WORLD DOESN'T END
UNENDING BLUES
WEATHER FORECAST FOR UTOPIA AND VICINITY
SELECTED POEMS 1963–1983
AUSTERITIES
CLASSIC BALLROOM DANCES
CHARON'S COSMOLOGY
RETURN TO A PLACE LIT BY A GLASS OF MILK
DISMANTLING THE SILENCE

Frightening Toys

◇

CHARLES SIMIC

faber and faber
LONDON · BOSTON

This collection first published in 1995
by Faber and Faber Limited
3 Queen Square London WC1N 3AU

Photoset by Wilmaset Ltd, Wirral
Printed in England by Clays Ltd, St Ives plc

All rights reserved

© Charles Simic, 1985, 1986, 1987, 1988, 1989, 1990, 1992, 1995

Charles Simic is hereby identified as author of this work in accordance with
Section 77 of the Copyright, Designs and Patents Act 1988

*This book is sold subject to the condition that it shall not, by way of trade
or otherwise, be lent, resold, hired out or otherwise circulated without the
publisher's prior consent in any form of binding or cover other than that
in which it is published and without a similar condition including
this condition being imposed on the subsequent purchaser*

A CIP record for this book is available from the British Library

ISBN 0-571-17399-3

2 4 6 8 10 9 7 5 3 1

Contents

[vii]

December

It snows
and still the derelicts
    go
carrying sandwich boards –

    one proclaiming
the end of the world
    the other
the rates of a local barbershop

The Marvels of the City

for Bata

I went down the tree-lined street of false gods
The cobbled street of two wise monkeys
The street of roasted nightingales
The small twisted street of the insomniacs
The street of those who feather their beds

That's right – the street of the dog's metaphysics
The dark alley of the Emperor's favorite barber
With its fountain and stone lion
The closed shutters on the street of the hundred-year-old harlot
The flag-bedecked courthouses and banks
On the square of the betrayed revolution

Here at last I thought feeling a rush of blood
The street of eternal recurrence and its proof
The tavern at the sign of the Pig and Seraphim
Erudite salamanders sipping wine of arctic vintage
Hamlet's wine the wine of stargazers
Loveless couples the wine of idiot savants

We are solely of the mind said one
Beyond Good and Evil said another
But the waiters black hair growing out of their ears
Just took our orders and said nothing

The Implements of Augury

for Ljubinka

Something like an empty chair and table
In a fortune-teller's storefront.
The Madame herself withdrawn from view,
Leaving us the dimly lit lampshade . . .

Most certainly, bequeathing to our care:
The empty street, the late hour,
The flowered tablecloth with tassels,
A neat pack of cards face down

In a huge nightbound city
Of many churches, hospitals,
Prisons and high tribunals
All equally deserted now.

The Madame herself withdrawn from view.
The cards as they were. The lampshade
With its flying mermaids and dragons,
The smiling mermaids, the fire-spitting dragons.

Early Evening Algebra

The madwoman went marking X's
With a piece of school chalk
On the backs of unsuspecting
Hand-holding, homebound couples.

It was winter. It was dark already.
One could not see her face
Bundled up as she was and furtive.
She went as if wind-swept, as if crow-winged.

The chalk must have been given to her by a child.
One kept looking for him in the crowd,
Expecting him to be very pale, very serious,
With a chip of black slate in his pocket.

William and Cynthia

Says she'll take him to the Museum
Of Dead Ideas and Emotions.
Wonders that he hasn't been there yet.
Says it looks like a Federal courthouse
With its many steps and massive columns.

Apparently not many people go there
On such drizzly gray afternoons.
Says even she gets afraid
In the large empty exhibition halls
With monstrous ideas in glass cases,
Naked emotions on stone pedestals
In classically provocative poses.

Says she doesn't understand why he claims
All that reminds him of a country fair.
Admits there's a lot of old dust
And the daylight is the color of sepia,
Just like on this picture postcard
With its two lovers chastely embracing
Against a painted cardboard sunset.

For the Sake of Amelia

Tending a cliff-hanging Grand Hotel
In a country ravaged by civil war.
My heart as its only bellhop.
My brain as its Chinese cook.

It's a run-down seaside place
With a row of gutted limousines out front,
Monkeys and fighting cocks in the great ballroom,
Potted palm trees grown wild to the ceilings.

Amelia surrounded by her beaus and fortune-tellers,
Painting her eyelashes and lips blue
In the hour of dusk with the open sea beyond,
The long empty beaches, the tide's shimmer . . .

She pleading with me to check the ledgers,
Find out if Lenin stayed here once,
Buster Keaton, Nathaniel Hawthorne,
St Bernard of Clairvaux, who wrote on love?

A hotel in which one tangos to a silence
Which has the look of cypresses in silent films . . .
In which children confide to imaginary friends . . .
In which pages of an important letter are flying . . .

But now a buzz from the suite with mirrors.
Amelia in the nude, black cotton over her eyes.
It seems there's a fly
On the tip of her lover's Roman nose.

Night of distant guns, distant and comfortable.
I am coming with a fly-swatter on a silver tray.
Ah the Turkish delights!
And the Mask of Tragedy over her pubic hair.

For the Lovers of the Absolute

A skinny arm thrown under
Her short-cropped head;
Then the penciled eyebrows,
Lips of a very serious child.

Naked and stretching herself
As if still convulsed
By passionate embraces –
Knees raised, thighs open
For a peek at the luxurious
Growth of black curls,

Glistening. The man by her side
With eyes shut. Broad chest,
Adam's apple rising evenly.
Already asleep – mouth open.
One long finely tapered hand
Cupping his sex as if in pain.

Still, instead of snores she hears
The distant artillery fire
That makes the blinds rattle
Ever so slightly; her breasts
Turn that ugly gooseflesh color –
And then she's fast asleep herself.

At the Night Court

You've combed yourself carefully,
Your Honor, with a small fine-tooth comb
You then cleverly concealed
Before making your entrance
In the splendor of your black robes.

The comb tucked inside a handkerchief
Scented with the extract of dead roses –
While you took your high seat
Sternly eyeing each of the accused
In the hush of the empty courtroom.

The dark curly hairs in the comb
Did not come from your graying head.
One of the cleaning women used it on herself
While you dozed off in your chambers
Half undressed because of the heat.

The black comb in the pocket over the heart,
You feel it tremble just as ours do
When they ready themselves to make music
Lacking only the paper you're signing,
By the looks of it, with eyes closed.

Popular Mechanics

The enormous engineering problems
You'll encounter by attempting to crucify yourself
Without helpers, pulleys, cogwheels,
And other clever mechanical contrivances –

In a small, bare, white room
With only a loose-legged chair
To reach the height of the ceiling –
Only a shoe to beat the nails in.

Not to mention being naked for the occasion –
So that each rib and muscle shows.
Your left hand already spiked in,
Only the right to wipe the sweat with,

To help yourself to a butt
From the overflowed ashtray,
You won't quite manage to light –
And the night coming, the whiz night.

In the Alley

You, with an earring, who diligently
Tattoo a bird of paradise
On the scrawny chest of a young sailor,
Didn't you notice it kept on snowing

Far into the night? While you labored
Over the colorful and ornate plumage
Of the exotic bird, and the beardless one
Sat shivering naked to the waist.

The great towers of Banking and Industry
Theatrically veiled and dimmed . . .
The grated shopwindows with their mannequins
Heads inclined as if overhearing things . . .

The heavy mirror you're tilting
For an admiring view
Of the spread wings, the wide-open beak
Triumphant — where the heart was!

Department of Public Monuments

If Justice and Liberty
Can be raised to pedestals,
Why not History?

It could be that fat woman
In faded overalls
Outside a house trailer
On a muddy road to some place called Pittsfield or Babylon.

She draws the magic circle
So the chickens can't get out,
Then she hobbles to the kitchen
For the knife and pail.

Today she's back carrying
A sack of yellow corn.
You can hear the hens cluck,
The dogs rattle their chains.

A Place in the Country

How well these dogs and their fleas
Know me and my black hat, not to mention
That fine collection of deathbeds upstairs.
How happy must be the frying pan

I take off its antique wrought-iron hook,
And the spoons which spent so much time
In the dark drawer, so that now
They look at the world wild-eyed.

They like me even better when
I eat too much and stretch on the floor.
Even the dust knows me then, and of course,
The wedding photographs on the wall.

What wouldn't they do for me, these long-departed
  couples!
At times the grandmothers strip naked,
And the men weep since we are at home,
And the fire is roaring in the stove,

While up above in what are still called the heavens,
There's our own chimney smoke
Like an old-time coachman's whip
For both the good and the bad angels.

Tidbit

He stuck his nose
Into the evening paper.
Got to have my glasses.
Where did I put them?

Where you left them,
Said she. Go shuffle
In the dark, grope
On table and sofa.

Not thinking to turn on
The lights. Save,
Save's all I hear,
Hard of hearing as I am.

Well, mister, I give up!
Both of them at a loss,
What next? And the paper
Sliding, sliding to the floor.

Outside a Dirtroad Trailer

O exegetes, somber hermeneuts,
Ingenious untanglers of ambiguities,
A bald little man was washing
The dainty feet of a very fat woman.

In a chair under a soaring shade tree,
She kept giggling and shaking her huge breasts.
There was also a boy with glasses
Engrossed in a book of serious appearance.

One black sock drying on the line,
A parked hearse with trash cans in the back,
And a large flag hanging limp from the pole
On a day as yet unproclaimed as a holiday.

To Helen

Tomorrow early I'm going to the doctor
In the blue suit and shirt you ironed.
Tomorrow I'm having my bones photographed
With my heart in its spiked branches.

It will look like a bird's nest in autumn
On a bleak day, one foot into the evening.
The tree is ill-shapen and alone in a field.
It must have been an apple, a crab apple

Tough and sour to make each tooth sore,
So that one goes off regretting, for now
The road's dark and there are new worries,
Fast swerving cars without headlights on,

Unknown drivers asleep at the wheel.
Because it's such a fine bone-chilling night.
Shadowy women are stirring black coffee,
Or they come out on the road to wait,

Wind-twisted and exquisitely blurred
In the wake of these cars that are moving
So fast or so slow, one barely hears them.
They're like clouds, if you hear them, the dark clouds.

Painters of Angels and Seraphim

After a long lunch of roast lamb
And many heavy glasses of heavy red wine,
I fell asleep in a rowboat
That I never got around to untie
From its mooring under the willows
That went on fussing over my head
As if to make my shade even deeper.

I woke once to pull my shirt off,
And once when I heard my name
Called by a woman, distant and worried,
Since it was past sundown,
The water reflecting the dark hills,
And the sky of that chill blue
That used to signify a state of grace.

Ancient Autumn

Is that foolish youth still sawing
The good branch he's sitting on?
Do the orchard and hill wheeze because of it,
And the few remaining apples sway?
Can he see the village in the valley
The way a chicken hawk would?

Already the pale plumes of woodsmoke scatter.
The days are getting short and chilly.
Even he must rest from time to time,
So he's lit a long-stemmed pipe
To watch a chimney sweep at work
And a woman pin diapers on the line
And then go behind some bushes,
Hike her skirts so that a bit of whiteness shows,
While on the commons humpbacked men
Roll a barrel of hard cider or beer,
And still beyond, past grazing cattle
Children play soldiers and march in step.

He figures, if the wind changes direction
He'll hear them shouting commands,
But it doesn't, so the black horseman
On the cobble of the road remains inaudible.
One instant he seems to be coming,
In the next to be leaving forever in a hurry . . .

It's these dumb shows with their vague lessons
That make him thoughtful and melancholy.
He's not even aware that he has resumed sawing,
That the big red sun is about to set.

Against Whatever It Is that's Encroaching

Best of all is to be idle,
And especially on a Thursday,
And to sip wine while studying the light:
The way it ages, yellows, turns ashen
And then hesitates forever
On the threshold of the night
That could be bringing the first frost.

It's good to have a woman around just then,
And two is even better.
Let them whisper to each other
And eye you with a smirk.
Let them roll up their sleeves and unbutton their shirts a bit
As this fine old twilight deserves,

And the small schoolboy
Who has come home to a room almost dark
And now watches wide-eyed
The grown-ups raise their glasses to him,
The giddy-headed, red-haired woman
With eyes tightly shut,
As if she were about to cry or sing.

First Frost

The time of the year for the mystics.
October sky and the Cloud of Unknowing.
The routes of eternity beckoning.
Sign and enigma in the humblest of things.

Master cobbler Jakob Boehme
Sat in our kitchen all morning.
He sipped tea and warned of the quiet
To which the wise must school themselves.

The young woman paid no attention.
Hair fallen over her eyes,
Breasts loose and damp in her robe,
Stubbornly scrubbing a difficult stain.

Then the dog's bark brought us all outdoors,
And that wasn't just geese honking,
But Dame Julian of Norwich herself discoursing
On the marvelous courtesy and homeliness of the
    Maker.

Without a Sough of Wind

Against the backdrop
Of a twilight world
In which one has done so little
For one's soul

She hangs a skirt
On the doorknob
She puts a foot on the chair
To take off a black stocking

And it's good to have eyes
Just then for the familiar
Large swinging breasts
And the cleft of her ass

Before the recital
Of that long day's
Woes and forebodings
In the warm evening

With the drone of insects
On the window screen
And the lit dial of a radio
Providing what light there is

Its sound turned much too low
To make out the words
Of what could be
A silly old love song

SCALIGER TURNS DEADLY pale at the sight of watercress. Tycho Brahe, the famous astronomer, passes out at the sight of a caged fox. Maria de Medici feels instantly giddy on seeing a rose, even in a painting. My ancestors, meanwhile, are eating cabbage. They keep stirring the pot looking for a pigfoot which isn't there. The sky is blue. The nightingale sings in a Renaissance sonnet, and immediately someone goes to bed with a toothache.

◇

I WAS STOLEN by the gypsies. My parents stole me right back. Then the gypsies stole me again. This went on for some time. One minute I was in the caravan suckling the dark teat of my new mother, the next I sat at the long dining room table eating my breakfast with a silver spoon.

It was the first day of spring. One of my fathers was singing in the bathtub; the other one was painting a live sparrow the colors of a tropical bird.

◇

I AM THE last Napoleonic soldier. It's almost two hundred years later and I am still retreating from Moscow. The road is lined with white birch trees and the mud comes up to my knees. The one-eyed woman wants to sell me a chicken, and I don't even have any clothes on.

The Germans are going one way; I am going the other. The Russians are going still another way and waving good-by. I have a ceremonial saber. I use it to cut my hair, which is four feet long.

◇

IT WAS THE epoch of the masters of levitation. Some evenings we saw solitary men and women floating above the dark tree tops. Could they have been sleeping or thinking? They made no attempt to navigate. The wind nudged them ever so slightly. We were afraid to speak, to breathe. Even the nightbirds were quiet. Later, we'd mention the little book clasped in the hands of the young woman, and the way that old man lost his hat to the cypresses.

In the morning there were not even clouds in the sky. We saw a few crows preen themselves at the edge of the road; the shirts raise their empty sleeves on the blind woman's clothesline.

History Lesson

The roaches look like
Comic rustics
In serious dramas.

◇

IN A FOREST of question marks you were no bigger than an asterisk.

O the season of mists! Someone blew the hunting horn.

The dictionary said you were a sign indicating an omission; then it changed the subject abruptly and spoke of 'asterisms', which supposedly have to do with crystals showing a starlike luminous figure.

You didn't believe a word of it. The question marks had valentines carved on their trunks so you wouldn't look up and notice the ropes.

Greasy ropes with baby nooses.

◇

HE CALLS ONE dog Rimbaud and the other Hölderlin. They are both mongrels. 'The unexamined life is not worth living' is his favorite saying. His wife looks like Delacroix's half-naked *Liberty*. She wears cowboy boots, picks dangerous-looking mushrooms in the forest. Tonight they will light tall candles and drink wine. Later, they'll open the door for the dogs to come in and eat the scraps under the table. 'Entrez, mes enfants!' he'll shout into the night, bowing deeply from the waist.

◇

A POEM ABOUT sitting on a New York rooftop on a chill autumn evening, drinking red wine, surrounded by tall buildings, the little kids running dangerously to the edge, the beautiful girl everyone's secretly in love with sitting by herself. She will die young but we don't know that yet. She has a hole in her black stocking, big toe showing, toe painted red . . . And the skyscrapers . . . in the failing light . . . like new Chaldeans, pythonesses, Cassandras . . . because of their many blind windows.

◇

ARE RUSSIAN CANNIBALS worse than the English? Of course. The English eat only the feet, the Russians the soul. 'The soul is a mirage,' I told Anna Alexandrovna, but she went on eating mine anyway.

'Like a superb confit of duck, or like a sparkling littleneck clam still in its native brine?' I inquired. But she just rubbed her belly and smiled at me from across the table.

◇

MY GUARDIAN ANGEL is afraid of the dark. He pretends he's not, sends me ahead, tells me he'll be along in a moment. Pretty soon I can't see a thing. 'This must be the darkest corner of heaven,' someone whispers behind my back. It turns out her guardian angel is missing too. 'It's an outrage,' I tell her. 'The dirty little cowards leaving us all alone,' she whispers. And of course, for all we know, I might be a hundred years old already, and she just a sleepy little girl with glasses.

THE OLD FARMER in overalls hanging from a barn beam. The cows looking sideways. The old woman kneeling under his swaying feet in her Sunday black dress and touching the ground with her forehead like a Mohammedan. Outside the sky is full of sudsy clouds above an endless plowed field with no other landmarks in view.

M.

I went on foot to M.
There was no one in M.

I had to tread softly
Past the house of cards –
A whole row of them
Thinking of falling down

In M. at the break of day.

◇

A CENTURY OF gathering clouds. Ghost ships arriving and leaving. The sea deeper, vaster. The parrot in the bamboo cage spoke several languages. The captain in the daguerreotype had his cheeks painted red. He brought a half-naked girl from the tropics whom they kept chained in the attic even after his death. At night she made sounds that could have been singing. The captain told of a race of men without mouths who subsisted only on scents of flowers. This made his wife and mother say a prayer for the salvation of all unbaptized souls. Once, however, we caught the captain taking off his beard. It was false! Under it he had another beard equally absurd looking.

It was the age of busy widows' walks. The dead languages of love were still in use, but also much silence, much soundless screaming at the top of the lungs.

◇

The time of minor poets is coming. Good-by Whitman,
Dickinson, Frost. Welcome you whose fame will never reach
beyond your closest family, and perhaps one or two good
friends gathered after dinner over a jug of fierce red wine . . .
while the children are falling asleep and complaining about the
noise you're making as you rummage through the closets for
your old poems, afraid your wife might've thrown them out
with last spring's cleaning.

It's snowing, says someone who has peeked into the dark
night, and then he, too, turns towards you as you prepare
yourself to read, in a manner somewhat theatrical and with a
face turning red, the long rambling love poem whose final
stanza (unknown to you) is hopelessly missing.

– after Aleksandar Ristović

◇

LOTS OF PEOPLE around here have been taken for rides in UFOs. You wouldn't think that possible with all the pretty white churches in sight so well-attended on Sundays.

'The round square doesn't exist,' says the teacher to the dull-witted boy. His mother was abducted only last night. All expectations to the contrary, she sits in the corner grinning to herself. The sky is vast and blue.

'They're so small, they can sleep inside their own ears,' says one eighty-year-old twin to the other.

O THE GREAT God of Theory, he's just a pencil stub, a chewed stub with a worn eraser at the end of a huge scribble.

◇

My father loved the strange books of André Breton. He'd raise the wine glass and toast those far-off evenings 'when butterflies formed a single uncut ribbon'. Or we'd go out for a piss in the back alley and he'd say: 'Here are some binoculars for blindfolded eyes.' We lived in a rundown tenement that smelled of old people and their pets.

'Hovering on the edge of the abyss, permeated with the perfume of the forbidden,' we'd take turns cutting the smoked sausage on the table. 'I love America,' he'd tell us. We were going to make a million dollars manufacturing objects we had seen in dreams that night.

◇

HE HAD MIXED up the characters in the long novel he was writing. He forgot who they were and what they did. A dead woman reappeared when it was time for dinner. A door-to-door salesman emerged out of a backwoods trailer wearing Chinese robes. The day the murderer was supposed to be electrocuted, he was buying flowers for a certain Rita, who turned out to be a ten-year-old girl with thick glasses and braids . . . And so it went.

He never did anything for me, though. I kept growing older and grumpier, as I was supposed to, in a ratty little town which he always described as 'dead' and 'near nothing'.

◇

SOMEONE SHUFFLES BY my door muttering: 'Our goose is cooked.'

Strange! I have my knife and fork ready. I even have the napkin tied around my neck, but the plate before me is still empty.

Nevertheless, someone continues to mutter outside my door regarding a certain hypothetical, allegedly cooked goose that he claims is ours in common.

The Little Pins of Memory

There was a child's Sunday suit
Pinned to a tailor's dummy
In a dusty store window.
The store looked closed for years.

I lost my way there once
In a Sunday kind of quiet,
Sunday kind of afternoon light
On a street of red-brick tenements.

How do you like that?
I said to no one.
How do you like that?
I said it again today upon waking.

That street went on forever
And all along I could feel the pins
In my back, prickling
The dark and heavy cloth.

St Thomas Aquinas

I left parts of myself everywhere
The way absent-minded people leave
Gloves and umbrellas
Whose colors are sad from dispensing so much back luck.

I was on a park bench asleep.
It was like the Art of Ancient Egypt.
I didn't wish to bestir myself.
I made my long shadow take the evening train.

'We give death to a child when we give it a doll,'
Said the woman who had read Djuna Barnes.
We whispered all night. She had traveled to darkest Africa.
She had many stories to tell about the jungle.

I was already in New York looking for work.
It was raining as in the days of Noah.
I stood in many doorways of that great city.
Once I asked a man in a tuxedo for a cigarette.
He gave me a frightened look and stepped out into the rain.

Since 'man naturally desires happiness,'
According to St Thomas Aquinas,
Who gave irrefutable proof of God's existence and purpose,
I loaded trucks in the Garment Center.
Me and a black man stole a woman's red dress.
It was of silk; it shimmered.

Upon a gloomy night with all our loving ardors on fire,
We carried it down the long empty avenue,
Each holding one sleeve.
The heat was intolerable causing many terrifying human faces
To come out of hiding.

In the Public Library Reading Room
There was a single ceiling fan barely turning.
I had the travels of Herman Melville to serve me as a pillow.
I was on a ghost ship with its sails fully raised.
I could see no land anywhere.
The sea and its monsters could not cool me.

I followed a saintly-looking nurse into a doctor's office.
We edged past people with eyes and ears bandaged.
'I am a medieval philosopher in exile,'
I explained to my landlady that night.
And, truly, I no longer looked like myself.
I wore glasses with a nasty spider crack over one eye.

I stayed in the movies all day long.
A woman on the screen walked through a bombed city
Again and again. She wore army boots.
Her legs were long and bare. It was cold wherever she was.
She had her back turned to me, but I was in love with her.
I expected to find wartime Europe at the exit.

It wasn't even snowing! Everyone I met
Wore a part of my destiny like a carnival mask.
'I'm Bartleby the Scrivener,' I told the Italian waiter.
'Me, too,' he replied.
And I could see nothing but overflowing ashtrays
The human-faced flies were busy examining.

A Letter

Dear philosophers, I get sad when I think.
Is it the same with you?
Just as I'm about to sink my teeth into the noumenon,
Some old girlfriend comes to distract me.
'She's not even alive!' I yell to the skies.

The wintry light made me go that way.
I saw beds covered with identical gray blankets.
I saw grim-looking men holding a naked woman
While they hosed her with cold water.
Was that to calm her nerves, or was it punishment?

I went to visit my friend Bob who said to me:
'We reach the real by overcoming the seduction of
    images.'
I was overjoyed, until I realized
Such abstinence will never be possible for me.
I caught myself looking out the window.

Bob's father was taking their dog for a walk.
He moved with pain; the dog waited for him.
There was no one else in the park,
Only bare trees with an infinity of tragic shapes
To make thinking difficult.

Factory

The machines were gone, and so were those who worked them.
A single high-backed chair stood like a throne
In all that empty space.
I was on the floor making myself comfortable
For a long night of little sleep and much thinking.

An empty bird cage hung from a steam pipe.
In it I kept an apple and a small paring knife.
I placed newspapers all around me on the floor
So I could jump at the slightest rustle.
It was like the scratching of a pen,
The silence of the night writing in its diary.

Of rats who came to pay me a visit
I had the highest opinion.
They'd stand on two feet
As if about to make a polite request
On a matter of great importance.

Many other strange things came to pass.
Once a naked woman climbed on the chair
To reach the apple in the cage.
I was on the floor watching her go on tiptoe,
Her hand fluttering in the cage like a bird.

On other days, the sun peeked through dusty windowpanes.
To see what time it was. But there was no clock,
Only the knife in the cage, glinting like a mirror,
And the chair in the far corner
Where someone once sat facing the brick wall.

Shelley

for M. Follain

Poet of the dead leaves driven like ghosts,
Driven like pestilence-stricken multitudes,
I read you first
One rainy evening in New York City,

In my atrocious Slavic accent,
Saying the mellifluous verses
From a battered, much-stained volume
I had bought earlier that day
In a second-hand bookstore on Fourth Avenue
Run by an initiate of the occult masters.

The little money I had being almost spent,
I walked the streets my nose in the book.
I sat in a dingy coffee shop
With last summer's dead flies on the table.
The owner was an ex-sailor
Who had grown a huge hump on his back
While watching the rain, the empty street.
He was glad to have me sit and read.
He'd refill my cup with a liquid dark as river Styx.

Shelley spoke of a mad, blind, dying king;
Of rulers who neither see, nor feel, nor know;
Of graves from which a glorious Phantom may
Burst to illumine our tempestuous day.

I too felt like a glorious phantom
Going to have my dinner
In a Chinese restaurant I knew so well.
It had a three-fingered waiter
Who'd bring my soup and rice each night
Without ever saying a word.

I never saw anyone else there.
The kitchen was separated by a curtain
Of glass beads which clicked faintly
Whenever the front door opened.
The front door opened that evening
To admit a pale little girl with glasses.

The poet spoke of the everlasting universe
Of things . . . of gleams of a remoter world
Which visit the soul in sleep . . .
Of a desert peopled by storms alone . . .

The streets were strewn with broken umbrellas
Which looked like funereal kites
This little Chinese girl might have made.
The bars on MacDougal Street were emptying.
There had been a fist fight.
A man leaned against a lamp post arms extended as if crucified,
The rain washing the blood off his face.

In a dimly lit side street,
Where the sidewalk shone like a ballroom mirror
At closing time —
A well-dressed man without any shoes
Asked me for money.
His eyes shone, he looked triumphant
Like a fencing master
Who had just struck a mortal blow.

How strange it all was . . . The world's raffle
That dark October night . . .
The yellowed volume of poetry
With its Splendors and Glooms
Which I studied by the light of storefronts:
Drugstores and barbershops,
Afraid of my small windowless room
Cold as a tomb of an infant emperor.

Two Dogs

for Charles and Holly

An old dog afraid of his own shadow
In some Southern town.
The story told me by a woman going blind,
One fine summer evening
As shadows were creeping
Out of the New Hampshire woods,
A long street with just a worried dog
And a couple of dusty chickens,
And all that sun beating down
In that nameless Southern town.

It made me remember the Germans marching
Past our house in 1944.
The way everybody stood on the sidewalk
Watching them out of the corner of the eye,
The earth trembling, death going by . . .
A little white dog ran into the street
And got entangled with the soldiers' feet.
A kick made him fly as if he had wings.
That's what I keep seeing!
Night coming down. A dog with wings.

Le Beau Monde

A man got up to talk about Marcel Proust,
'The great French writer',
From a soapbox famous for its speeches
About crooked bosses and the working poor.

I swear it (Tony Russo is my witness).
It was late one night, the crowd was thinning,
But then they all came back
To see what his mumbling was all about.

He looked like a dishwasher
From one of the dives on Avenue B.
He chewed his nails as he spoke.
He said this and that in what must've been French.

Everybody perked up, even the winos.
The tough guys stopped flexing their muscles.
It was like being in church
When the High Mass was said in Latin.

Nobody had a clue, but it made you feel good.
When it was over, he just walked away,
Long-legged and in a big hurry.
The rest of us taking our time to disperse.

The Betrothal

I found a key
In the street, someone's
House key
Lying there, glinting,

Long ago; the one
Who lost it
Is not going to remember it
Tonight, as I do.

It was a huge city
Of many dark windows,
Columns and domes.
I stood there thinking.

The street ahead of me
Shadowy, full of peril
Now that I held
The key. One or two

Late strollers
Unhurried and grave
In view. The sky above them
Of an unearthly clarity.

Eternity jealous
Of the present moment,
It occurred to me!
And then the moment was over.

Frightening Toys

History practicing its scissor-clips
In the dark,
So everything comes out in the end
Missing an arm or a leg.

Still, if that's all you've got
To play with today . . .
This doll at least had a head,
And its lips were red!

Frame houses like grim exhibits
Lining the empty streets
Where a little girl sat on the steps
In a flowered nightgown, talking to it.

It looked like a serious matter,
Even the rain wanted to hear about it,
So it fell on her eyelashes,
And made them glisten.

The Big War

We played war during the war,
Margaret. Toy soldiers were in big demand,
The kind made from clay.
The lead ones they melted into bullets, I suppose.

You never saw anything as beautiful
As those clay regiments! I used to lie on the floor
For hours staring them in the eye.
I remember them staring back at me in wonder.

How strange they must have felt
Standing stiffly at attention
Before a large, incomprehending creature
With a moustache made of milk.

In time they broke, or I broke them on purpose.
There was wire inside their limbs,
Inside their chests, but nothing in the heads!
Margaret, I made sure.

Nothing at all in the heads . . .
Just an arm, now and then, an officer's arm,
Wielding a saber from a crack
In my deaf grandmother's kitchen floor.

The White Room

The obvious is difficult
To prove. Many prefer
The hidden. I did, too.
I listened to the trees.

They had a secret
Which they were about to
Make known to me,
And then didn't.

Summer came. Each tree
On my street had its own
Scheherazade. My nights
Were a part of their wild

Story-telling. We were
Entering dark houses,
More and more dark houses
Hushed and abandoned.

There was someone with eyes closed
On the upper floors.
The thought of it, and the wonder,
Kept me sleepless.

The truth is bald and cold,
Said the woman
Who always wore white.
She didn't leave her room much.

The sun pointed to one or two
Things that had survived
The long night intact,
The simplest things,

Difficult in their obviousness.
They made no noise.
It was the kind of day
People describe as 'perfect'.

Gods disguising themselves
As black hairpins? A hand-mirror?
A comb with a tooth missing?
No! That wasn't it.

Just things as they are,
Unblinking, lying mute
In that bright light,
And the trees waiting for the night.

Celestial Overseers

Do they count my steps meticulously?
Have they reached a figure
Of many zeros separated by commas?
Could I have walked to the nearest star already?

Recall for me, please,
One of my first steps.
I want the suit I was wearing that day pressed.
I want my mother to hold my hand tightly.

That must be our grandmother there
In the open coffin. Her hands are chapped
From scrubbing so much
The floor we walk on in black shoes.

The three little steps I took then
So that I might be lifted up to kiss her,
And the three equally tiny ones to withdraw . . .
Do they still resound at ever-receding magnitudes?

Could this large dog sitting sphinxlike
By the gray Atlantic shore
Still hear my new shoes squeaking
On the other side of the world?

The Pieces of the Clock Lie Scattered

So, hurry up!
The evening's coming.
The grown-ups are on the way.
There'll be hell to pay.

You forgot about time
While you sought its secret
In the slippery wheels,
Some of which had teeth.

You meant to enthrall
The girl across the hall.
She drew so near,
Her breast brushed your ear.

She ought to have gone home,
But you kept telling her
You'll have it together again
And ticking in no time.

Instead, you're under the table
Together, searching the floor.
Your hands are trembling,
And there's a key in the door.

At the Corner

The fat sisters
Kept a candy store
Dim and narrow
With dusty jars
Of jaw-breaking candy.

We stayed thin, stayed
Glum, chewing gum
While staring at the floor,
The shoes of many strangers
Rushing in and out,

Making the papers outside
Flutter audibly
Under the lead weights,
Their headlines
Screaming in and out of view.

The World

As if I were a big old shade tree
On a side street with a small café.
Neon beer sign with the word 'cold' shining in it.
Summer dusk.

The solitary customer, who looks like my father,
Is bent over a book with small print
Oblivious of the young waiter
Who is about to serve him a cup of black coffee.

I have an incalculable number of leaves
Not one of which is moving.
It's because we are enchanted, I think.
We don't have a care in the world.

Cabbage

She was about to chop the head
In half,
But I made her reconsider
By telling her:
'Cabbage symbolizes mysterious love.'

Or so said one Charles Fourier,
Who said many other strange and wonderful things,
So that people called him mad behind his back,

Whereupon I kissed the back of her neck
Ever so gently,

Whereupon she cut the cabbage in two
With a single stroke of her knife.

Babylon

Every time I prayed
The universe got bigger,
And I got smaller.

My wife almost stepped on me.
I saw her huge legs
Rising to dizzying heights.
The hair between them
Glistened like a god's beard.
She looked Babylonian.

'I'm getting smaller every minute,'
I yelled, but she could not hear me
Among the winged lions and ziggurats,
The mad astrologers of her painted eyes.

The Wail

As if there were nothing to live for . . .
As if there were . . . nothing.
In the fading light, our mother
Sat sewing with her head bowed.

Did her hand tremble? By the first faint
Hint of night coming, how all lay
Still, except for the memory of that voice:
Him whom the wild life hurried away . . .

Long stretches of silence in between.
Clock talking to a clock.
Dogs lying on their paws with ears cocked.
You and me afraid to breathe.

Finally, she went to peek. Someone covered
With a newspaper on the sidewalk.
Otherwise, no one about. The street empty.
The sky full of gypsy clouds.

The Scarecrow

God's refuted but the devil's not.

This year's tomatoes are something to see.
Bite into them, Martha,
As you would into a ripe apple.
After each bite add a little salt.

If the juices run down your chin
Onto your bare breasts,
Bend over the kitchen sink.

From there you can see your husband
Come to a dead stop in the empty field
Before one of his bleakest thoughts
Spreading its arms like a scarecrow.

Windy Evening

This old world needs propping up
When it gets this cold and windy.
The cleverly painted sets,
Oh, they're shaking badly!
They're about to come down.

There'll be nothing but infinite space then.
The silence supreme. Almighty silence.
Egyptian sky. Stars like torches
Of grave robbers entering the crypts of the kings.
Even the wind pausing, waiting to see.

Better grab hold of that tree, Lucille.
Its shape crazed, terror-stricken.
I'll hold the barn.
The chickens in it uneasy.
Smart chickens, rickety world.

Fourteenth Street Poem

for Drena

The bag lady who shouted
She was Venus,
The Goddess of Love!
Had two front teeth missing.

It was a long block
Favored by doomsday prophets,
Blind street musicians,
Dogs licking their padlocks.

Photographs of missing children
Watched us meet and separate:
Me with a deep bow, her
With a finger on her lips
Making it 'our' secret.

The Congress of the Insomniacs

Mother of God, everyone is invited:
Stargazing Peruvian shepherds,
Old men on sidewalks of New York.
You, too, doll with eyes open
Listening to the rain next to a sleeping child.

A big hotel ballroom with mirrors on every side.
Think about it as you lie in the dark.
Angels on its ornate ceilings,
Naked nymphs in what must be paradise.

There's a stage, a lectern,
An usher with a flashlight.
Someone will address this gathering yet
From his bed of nails.
Sleeplessness is like metaphysics.
Be there.

The City

At least one crucified at every corner.
The eyes of a mystic, madman, murderer.
They know it's truly for nothing.
The eyes do. All the martyr's sufferings
On parade. Exalted mother of us all
Tending her bundles on the sidewalk,
Speaking to each as if it were a holy child.

There were many who saw none of this.
A couple lingered on kissing lustily
Right where someone lay under a newspaper.
His bloody feet, swollen twice their size,
Jutted out into the cold of the day,
Grim proofs of a new doctrine.

I tell you, I was afraid. A man screamed
And continued walking as if nothing had happened.
Everyone whose eyes I sought avoided mine.
Was I beginning to resemble him a little?
I had no answer to any of these questions.
Neither did the crucified on the next corner.

Stub of a Red Pencil

You were sharpened to a fine point
With a rusty razor blade.
Then the unknown hand swept the shavings
Into its moist palm
And disappeared from view.

You lay on the desk next to
The official-looking document
With a long list of names.
It was up to us to imagine the rest:
The high ceiling with its cracks
And odd-shaped water stains;
The window with its view
Of roofs covered with snow.

An inconceivable, varied world
Surrounding your severe presence
On every side,
Stub of a red pencil.

The Prodigal

Dark morning rain
Meant to fall
On a prison and a school yard,
Falling meanwhile
On my mother and her old dog.

How slow she shuffles now
In my father's Sunday shoes.
The dog by her side
Trembling with each step
As he tries to keep up.

I am on another corner waiting
With my head shaved.
My mind hops like a sparrow
In the rain.
I'm always watching and worrying about her.

Everything is a magic ritual,
A secret cinema,
The way she appears in a window hours later
To set the empty bowl
And spoon on the table,
And then exits
So that the day may pass,
And the night may fall
Into the empty bowl,
Empty room, empty house,
While the rain keeps
Knocking at the front door.

Hotel Insomnia

I liked my little hole,
Its window facing a brick wall.
Next door there was a piano.
A few evenings a month
A crippled old man came to play
'My Blue Heaven'.

Mostly, though, it was quiet.
Each room with its spider in heavy overcoat
Catching his fly with a web
Of cigarette smoke and revery.
So dark,
I could not see my face in the shaving mirror.

At 5 a.m. the sound of bare feet upstairs.
The 'Gypsy' fortune-teller,
Whose storefront is on the corner,
Going to pee after a night of love.
Once, too, the sound of a child sobbing.
So near it was, I thought
For a moment, I was sobbing myself.

Tragic Architecture

School, prison, trees in the wind,
I climbed your gloomy stairs,
Stood in your farthest corners
With my face to the wall.

The murderer sat in the front row.
A mad little Ophelia
Wrote today's date on the blackboard.
The executioner was my best friend.
He already wore black.
The janitor brought us mice to play with.

In that room with its red sunsets —
It was eternity's time to speak,
So we listened
As if our hearts were made of stone.

All of that in ruins now.
Cracked, peeling walls
With every window broken.
Not even a naked light bulb left
For the prisoner forgotten in solitary,
And the schoolboy left behind
Watching the bare winter trees
Lashed by the driving wind.

Makers of Labyrinths

I must be absolutely alone when I think,
And on the highest parapet
Overlooking the empty street.
The dusty store window down below
Is full of phantoms at sunset.

There goes my old man. He is already the age I am now.
With eyes closed
He calls the waiters by their secret names:
St Isaac, the Syrian,
St Nilus, who wrote on prayer.
The wine of eternal ambiguities,
If you please, to the health of the crow
Sitting on the top of a white church.

His life, too, is a fantastic maze.
Our misfortunes are builders.
They always forget about windows,
Make the ceilings low and heavy.
'It's only a paper moon,' they sing . . .
But I'm getting ahead of myself.

At the end of a dark corridor
There is a lit match in a trembling hand.
'I still have stage fright,'
The beautiful woman says,
And then she leads us past wardrobes
With mirrors and creaking doors
Where whispering dresses hang,
Whispering corsets, button shoes –
The kind you'd wear while riding a goat.

Her daughter, we are told, is consumptive.
There's a sign of death's greasy thumbprint
On her angelic face.
She wants me to play under the table
Of the silent card players.

We play and it's like the palace at Knossos.
Memory, my heart's only burnt match:
Her hand guiding me in the ruins,
And the cards whispering over our heads
Made giddy by our youth and our love.

The Inanimate Object

IN MY LONG late night talks with the jailers, I raised again the question of the object: Does it remain indifferent whether it is perceived or not? (I had in mind the one concealed and found posthumously while the newly vacated cell was fumigated and swept.)

'Like a carved-wood demon of some nightmarish species,' said one. 'In cipher writ,' said another. We were drinking a homemade brew that made our heads spin. 'When a neck button falls on the floor and hardly makes a sound,' said the third with a smile, but I said nothing.

'If only one could leave behind a little something to make others stop and think,' I thought to myself.

In the meantime, there was my piece of broken bottle to worry about. It was green and had a deadly cutting edge. I no longer remembered its hiding place, unless I had only dreamed of it, or this was another cell, another prison in an infinite series of prisons and long night talks with my jailers.

The Tiger

in memory of George Oppen

In San Francisco, that winter,
There was a dark little store
Full of sleepy Buddhas.
The afternoon I walked in,
No one came out to greet me.
I stood among the sages
As if trying to read their thoughts.

One was huge and made of stone.
A few were the size of a child's head
And had stains the color of dried blood.
There were even some no bigger than mice,
And they appeared to be listening.

'The winds of March, black winds,
The gritty winds,' the dead poet wrote.

At sundown his street was empty
Except for my long shadow
Open before me like scissors.
There was his house where I told the story
Of the Russian soldier,
The one who looked Chinese.

He lay wounded in my father's bed,
And I brought him water and matches.
For that he gave me a little tiger
Made of ivory. Its mouth was open in anger,
But it had no stripes left.

There was the night when I colored
Its eyes black, its tongue red.
My mother held the lamp for me,
While worrying about the kind of luck
This beast might bring us.

The tiger in my hand growled faintly
When we were alone in the dark,
But when I put my ear to the poet's door
That afternoon, I heard nothing.

'The winds of March, black winds,
The gritty winds,' he once wrote.

Clouds Gathering

It seemed the kind of life we wanted.
Wild strawberries and cream in the morning.
Sunlight in every room.
The two of us walking by the sea naked.

Some evenings, however, we found ourselves
Unsure of what comes next.
Like tragic actors in a theater on fire,
With birds circling over our heads,
The dark pines strangely still,
Each rock we stepped on bloodied by the sunset.

We were back on our terrace sipping wine.
Why always this hint of an unhappy ending?
Clouds of almost human appearance
Gathering on the horizon, but the rest lovely
With the air so mild and the sea untroubled.

The night suddenly upon us, a starless night.
You lighting a candle, carrying it naked
Into our bedroom and blowing it out quickly.
The dark pines and grasses strangely still.

Folk Songs

Sausage-makers of History,
The bloody kind,
You all hail from a village
Where the dog barking at the moon
Is the only poet.

*

O King Oedipus, O Hamlet,
Fallen like flies
In the pot of cabbage soup,
No use beating with your fists,
Or sticking your tongues out.

*

Christ-faced spider on the wall
Darkened by evening shadows,
I spent my childhood on a cross
In a yard full of weeds,
White butterflies, and white chickens.

A Book Full of Pictures

Father studied theology through the mail
And this was exam time.
Mother knitted. I sat quietly with a book
Full of pictures. Night fell.
My hands grew cold touching the faces
Of dead kings and queens.

There was a black raincoat in the upstairs bedroom
Swaying from the ceiling,
But what was it doing there?
Mother's long needles made quick crosses.
They were black
Like the inside of my head just then.

The pages I turned sounded like wings.
'The soul is a bird,' he once said.
In my book full of pictures
A battle raged: lances and swords
Made a kind of wintry forest
With my heart spiked and bleeding in its branches.

Hotel Starry Sky

Millions of empty rooms with TV sets turned on.
I wasn't there yet I saw everything.
Titanic on the screen like a birthday cake sinking.
Poseidon, the night clerk, blew out the candles.

How much should we tip the blind bellboy?
At three in the morning the gum machine in the empty lobby
With its freshly cracked mirror
Is the new Madonna with her infant child.

To Think Clearly

What I need is a pig and an angel.
The pig to stick his nose in a slop bucket,
The angel to scratch his back
And say sweet things in his ear.

The pig knows what's in store for him.
Give him hope, angel child,
With that foreverness stuff.
Don't go admiring yourself
In the butcher's knife
As if it were a whore's mirror,
Or tease him with a blood-stained apron
By raising it above your knees.

The pig has stopped eating
And stands among us thinking.
Already the crest of the rooster blazes
In the morning darkness.
He's not crowing but his eyes are fierce
As he struts across the yard.

The Chair

This chair was once a student of Euclid.

The book of his laws lay on its seat.
The schoolhouse windows were open,
So the wind turned the pages
Whispering the glorious proofs.

The sun set over the golden roofs.
Everywhere the shadows lengthened,
But Euclid kept quiet about that.

In the Night

The winds were making soup
For the insomniacs,

Weathervane soup.

True History

Which cannot be put into words –
Like a fly on the map of the world
In the travel agent's window.

That street empty in the afternoon heat
Except for my old father
Pressing his head against the glass
To observe her better
As she drags her threadbare shadow
From New York to Shanghai.

He not sure whether to alert his friend,
The barber, napping next door
With a sheet draped over his head.

Marina's Epic

The Eskimos were ravaging Peru.
Grandfather fought the Hittites.
Mother sold firecrackers to the Bedouins.

One night when the moon was full
She met the lion who ate Lev Tolstoy.

We were inmates of an orphanage in Cracow;
A prison in Panama;
A school for beggars in Genoa.

My sister insisted on rescuing ladybugs.
Down a succession of gloomy corridors
She carried the glistening and shivering creature
On the long nail of her index finger.

Our Fate was a crackpot inventor
Working in a garage.

In Paris I knew a Russian lady
Who scrubbed floors at the opera
With a rose between her teeth like Carmen.

Father played a dead man in a German movie.
It was silent. The piano player looked like
Edgar Allan Poe wearing a Moroccan fez.

We stood outside a pink motel in Arizona singing:
'We love you life
Even though you're always laughing at us.'

The next day I joined the Tibetans.
They had a holy mountain
From which one could see Los Angeles.

Sardinian goat cheese, Greek olives, Hungarian sausage
On the table –
Because memory makes you hungry.

On the back of a sleeping shark
We sailed the stormy Atlantic
Taking turns to mend the rips in grandmother's wedding dress
We used as a sail.

In America the movie screens were as big as the pyramids.

Broadway was a river like the Amazon.
Drowned heads popping up with eyes open:
Ophelias and Valentinos by the thousands.

In Japan they were catching ghosts
With chopsticks.
In Amsterdam there was a Christmas tree
In a whorehouse.

I stood on the corner with the Zulus.
We were waiting for fool's bells,
Gypsy woman's love potion,
General Washington to ride by on his horse
And nod in our direction.

Lost Glove

Here's a woman's black glove.
It ought to mean something.
A thoughtful stranger left it
On the red mailbox at the corner.

Three days the sky was troubled,
Then today a few snowflakes fell
On the glove, which someone,
In the meantime, had turned over,
So that its fingers could close

A little . . . Not yet a fist.
So I waited, with the night coming.
Something told me not to move.
Here where flames rise from trash barrels,
And the homeless sleep standing up.

Beauty

I'M TELLING YOU, this was the real thing, the same one they kicked out of Aesthetics, told her she didn't exist!

O you simple, indefinable, ineffable, and so forth. I like your black apron, and your new Chinese girl's hairdo. I also like naps in the afternoon, well-chilled white wine, and the squabbling of philosophers.

What joy and happiness you give us each time you reach over the counter to take our money, so we catch a whiff of your breath. You've been chewing on sesame crackers and garlic salami, divine creature!

When I heard the old man, Plotinus, say something about 'every soul wanting to possess you', I gave him a dirty look, and rushed home to unwrap and kiss the pink ham you sliced for me with your own hand.

Street Scene

A blind little boy
With a paper sign
Pinned to his chest.
Too small to be out
Begging alone,
But there he was.

This strange century
With its slaughter of the innocent,
Its flight to the moon —
And now he waiting for me
In a strange city,
On a street where I lost my way.

Hearing me approach,
He took a rubber toy
Out of his mouth
As if to say something,
But then he didn't.

It was a head, a doll's head,
Badly chewed,
Held high for me to see.
The two of them grinning at me.

My Quarrel with the Infinite

I preferred the fleeting,
Like a memory of a sip of wine
Of noble vintage
On the tongue with eyes closed . . .

When you tapped me on the shoulder,
O light, unsayable in your splendor.
A lot of good you did to me.
You just made my insomnia last longer.

I sat rapt at the spectacle,
Secretly ruing the fugitive:
All its provisory, short-lived
Kisses and enchantments.

Here with the new day breaking,
And a single scarecrow on the horizon
Directing the traffic
Of crows and their shadows.

Pyramids and Sphinxes

There's a street in Paris
Called rue des Pyramides.
Once I imagined it was lined
With sand and pyramids.

The Sunday I went there to make sure,
A poor old woman with a limp
Overtook me without looking my way.
She could've been Egyptian
Because of her advanced age.

Leaning on a cane and still hurrying
Past the shuttered storefronts
As if there was a parade somewhere,
Or an execution to see –
A bloody head held high by its hair!

The day was cold. She soon disappeared,
While I studied a peeling circus poster
Under which there was another
With the head of a sphinx staring at me.

The Artist

Do you remember the crazy guy
Who stuck candles in his hat
So he could paint the sea at night?
Alone on that empty Jersey beach,
He kept squinting into the dark,
And waving his brush wildly.

Theresa said he got the dumb idea
From a movie she saw once.
Still, there he was, bearded and hairy
Like the devil himself
Piling one murky color on top of another
While we stood around watching,
The candles on his head flickering
Then going out one by one.

The Old World

for Dan and Jeanne

I believe in the soul; so far
It hasn't made much difference.
I remember an afternoon in Sicily.
The ruins of some temple.
Columns fallen in the grass like naked lovers.

The olives and goat cheese tasted delicious
And so did the wine
With which I toasted the coming night,
The darting swallows,
The Saracen wind and moon.

It got darker. There was something
Long before there were words:
The evening meal of shepherds . . .
A fleeting whiteness among the trees . . .
Eternity eavesdropping on time.

The goddess going to bathe in the sea.
She must not be followed.
These rocks, these cypress trees,
May be her old lovers.
Oh to be one of them, the wine whispered to me.

Country Fair

for Hayden Carruth

If you didn't see the six-legged dog,
It doesn't matter.
We did and he mostly lay in the corner.
As for the extra legs,

One got used to them quickly
And thought of other things.
Like, what a cold, dark night
To be out at the fair.

Then the keeper threw a stick
And the dog went after it
On four legs, the other two flapping behind,
Which made one girl shriek with laughter.

She was drunk and so was the man
Who kept kissing her neck.
The dog got the stick and looked back at us.
And that was the whole show.